AF347208

Learn to Understand Others

N Chokkan

Learn to Understand Others

© *New Horizon Media*

First Edition: July 2011
64 Pages
Printed in India.

ISBN 978–81–8493–511–0
Pro–ya–en–88

Prodigy Books
177/103, First Floor, Ambal's Building
Lloyds Road, Royapettah, Chennai 600 014.
Ph: +91-44-4200-9601

Email: support@nhm.in
Website: www.nhm.in

Prodigy Books is an imprint of New Horizon Media Pvt. Ltd.

All rights relating to this work rest with the copyright holder. Except for reviews and quotations, use or republication of any part of this work is prohibited under the copyright act, without the prior written permission of the publisher of this book.

The World Health Organization has defined life skills as, 'the abilities for adaptive and positive behaviour that enable individuals to deal effectively with the demands and challenges of everyday life.'

Life skills are essentially those abilities that help promote mental well-being and competence in young people as they face the realities of life. With life skills, one is able to explore alternatives, and understand one's strengths and weaknesses.

Empathy is one of the ten core life skill strategies and techniques listed by WHO (World Health Organisation)

List of core life skill strategies and techniques listed by WHO

Effective communication

Creative thinking

Decision-making

Problem solving

Critical thinking

Interpersonal relationship skills

Self-awareness

Empathy

Coping with emotions

Coping with stress

The Race

It was the School Annual Day. All the children were very excited, especially those participating in various events and competitions such as sports, painting, singing, dancing and so on.

The school ground was abuzz with activity. Children were running around, in their white shorts and shirts, getting ready for the big event.

After a few minutes, there was a long whistle. Everyone took their positions, ready to run as soon as the signal was given.

The special guest for the day shot a dummy pistol, and the next second all the children started running as fast as possible, towards the shiny red ribbon at the other end of the race track.

From the very beginning, Shravan was in the lead... and a few paces behind him was Arun. The crowd cheered loudly, 'Come on Arun, you can make it!'

This excited Arun and he started running faster. Within a few seconds, he crossed Shravan and was leading the race. Shravan got annoyed and tried to overtake Arun. But he couldn't.

The crowd sat watching the stiff competition between Arun and Shravan. They were trying to outrun each other and everyone knew it was going to be a photo finish.

As they were nearing the finish line, Shravan fell down all of a sudden. No one knew what made him fall, but he was on the ground. Arun knew by instinct that something had gone wrong and Shravan needed help.

But was this the time to help Shravan? The race would be over within the next few seconds with Arun as the clear winner.

Arun didn't think that way. He stopped, turned around, ran towards Shravan and took him in his arms, 'Shravan, What happened? Are you hurt?'

Shravan couldn't speak. Arun helped Shravan get up. In the next few minutes, Shravan was given the first aid and someone took him to the nearby hospital.

Doctors confirmed that there was nothing serious and that Shravan would be back on track pretty soon.

But which track? The race was already over. Both Arun and Shravan have lost the race.

Shravan looked at Arun with gloomy eyes, 'You deserved to win,' he said, 'and because of me, you lost.'

'No Shravan, winning is not everything,' Arun said. 'I am very happy that I could help you and now you are alright. We can always win another race. Don't worry!'

Not only Shravan, everyone in the school was very surprised to hear what Arun had done. He sacrificed his #1 position in the race, to help his competitor. Why?

He could have helped Shravan after winning the race. Nothing would have gone wrong in a matter of few seconds. But there was a strong reason behind the way Arun reacted at that moment. He was empathetic.

Empathy? What is that?

Empathy is the ability to understand other people's feelings, emotions and problems. In other words, it is standing in someone else's shoes and looking at life through their reference point. It has many other deeper meanings and significance which we shall discuss later. For the moment, let's just analyse what Arun has done. He reacted differently to the situation, unlike the way you or I would have reacted. Why?

First of all, when Arun saw Shravan falling down, he didn't think of him as an enemy or as a competitor trying to snatch away his victory. He saw Shravan as a fellow-being.

In fact, he forgot all about the race. He forgot the fact that he was only few seconds away from the goal as his mind was occupied with the thought, 'I must do something to save Shravan… immediately!'

Normally, everyone thinks that the world revolves around them. This means they treat all others as secondary, resulting in a selfish 'I' and similar thoughts and actions.

Arun was empathetic and saw himself in Shravan. Hence, all his 'selfish' goals disappeared and he helped his friend.

Remember, it sounds very simple and obvious. But in reality, it's not very easy to think or act that way. We shall learn all about it in the next few chapters!

How Do I Feel?

In the previous chapter, we came across a few words like emotions and feelings. What are they?

It is difficult to describe these words, mainly because they don't have a form or a shape. We can't see them, or touch them; they are just felt, not by your fingers, but by your heart. That's why they are called feelings.

Typically, there are two kinds of feelings people experience: happiness and unhappiness. Feelings are languages we learn much before we speak or write in our mother tongue. For example, a baby cries if it is hungry, and smiles if it is happy.

The same holds true for adults too. When your mother asks you to do something and you refuse, she becomes unhappy (or angry). On the other hand, if you obey her and complete the work as instructed, she is all smiles and shows a happy face.

So, what does this mean? Clearly, our feelings are driven by the external world, or the people around us. We may not realise it, but it is happening every day, every moment.

Let us assume that you are walking towards your school and one of your schoolmate passes you in a cycle. You start to think, 'He has a cycle, but I am forced to walk to school everyday!'

What happened all of a sudden. You were walking to school happily and the appearance of your schoolmate in a cycle changed your feeling into a negative one.

Remember, that your schoolmate didn't talk to you. He didn't tease you about your walking to school. This feeling was born out of your own thought process.

Sometimes, others may force a feeling on you. Like the example below:

An aged saint was living in a jungle. The king of that country heard about this great man, and went to visit him. When the saint saw the king, he simply smiled. He asked the king, 'What brings you here?'

The king said, 'Oh great one, I have a doubt!'

'What is your doubt?'

'What is the difference between heaven and hell?'

Immediately, the saint's face changed, and he started shouting, 'Are you stupid? You call yourself a king, but you don't know the answer to this simple question? Shame on you!'

The king couldn't stand this insult and drew his sword to kill the saint.

The saint smiled again and said, 'Oh king, this anger will make you a violent animal. It is as good as facing hell on earth!'

The king realised his mistake, and dropped the sword. Now the saint said, 'This understanding will make you a better human being. It is as good as facing heaven on earth!'

In this story, the saint purposefully used some words to trigger the king's emotion (anger). He fell for them, and went to the extent of killing the saint. Fortunately, he didn't do so, and learnt an important lesson.

We interact with many people everyday. Each one of them would say something that triggers a feeling. We can't avoid this. But if we have the self-realisation of how we feel about something, it is a lot easier to control our emotions and act responsibly.

But how can we know what feeling/emotion we are in, at any given point of time? As we saw earlier, feelings are very personal. So, we don't need someone else to tell us how we feel, we should be able to realise it ourselves.

For that to happen, we should become more expressive in terms of conveying our feelings. As an example, consider these statements:

1a. I don't like this movie.

1b. I don't like this movie because it makes me feel scared.

2a. I love playing cricket.

2b. I love playing cricket because I enjoy scoring runs and taking wickets.

3a. I hate this weather.

3b. I hate this weather as I am not able to go out and play.

If you notice, the statements 1a, 2a and 3a convey a message. But 1b, 2b and 3b are more expressive.

What is the use in knowing how we feel? Is it so important?

Yes. Without realising our own feelings, we won't be able to understand how others feel.

A lady was constantly complaining about her neighbour to her husband, 'You know, those people are very dirty.'

'How do you say that?' asked the husband.

'Look at their house. It has so much of dust in it. If a family maintains the house like this, I am sure they will be the dirtiest people ever!'

The husband was annoyed at such generalisation and said, 'My dear, dust is not in their house but in our window glasses!'

True. After wiping the glasses, the neighbour's house looked very clean.

We generally commit the mistake of blaming our actions on someone else. But the truth may be that we are missing an emotion, or a feeling within us. Once we realise our own emotions, the next step will be to see how others feel. This is an important first step in the journey towards empathy!

Face It!

There are two aspects that help us understand others. First, observing them and realising how they feel, and then establishing trust and rapport.

For the moment, let us forget the second part (establishing trust and rapport). This will help us focus on the first aspect—observing—and understanding how others feel.

Understanding others' emotions is not easy. We need to practise a lot on this, otherwise our guess might go wrong and we may react in a totally unexpected way, causing misunderstandings and troubles.

When you are riding a bike, or a car, there is a speedometer which indicates the speed of the vehicle.

Similarly, there are other indicators that show us the fuel level, water level, distance travelled and so on.

Wouldn't it be nice if we have a similar indicator to gauge people's emotions too? Something which gives a red signal if they are angry and a green signal if they are happy!

Fortunately, there is one such indicator. It is called the face! Face?

Yes. Our face is the mirror of our mind and a good indicator of what we feel. Hence, we can use the same knowledge to judge others' emotions.

How?

Let us do a small test. Stand in front of a mirror, and show a 'happy face'. You don't need any more instructions. Because we all know how a happy face looks like. We may not realise it consciously, but when we are happy, our eyes look bright and our face is lit with a smile. On the other hand, when we are sad, these things happen in reverse.

Similarly, many other emotions can also be gauged from the facial expressions of other people. For example, anger, shyness, excitement, mischief and so on. In fact, there is a dedicated topic in psychology called 'Face

Reading' or 'Face Language' which helps us to learn people's emotions from their facial expressions. Let us learn a couple of simple exercises, to master this.

First, you need to go to a crowded place. Don't choose a place where people know you, instead opt for a public area like a railway station, or a temple, or a shopping mall, or a movie theatre.

In these places, you will see a lot of strangers. Look at their faces carefully and observe their facial expressions to guess if they are happy, or sad, or angry, and so on.

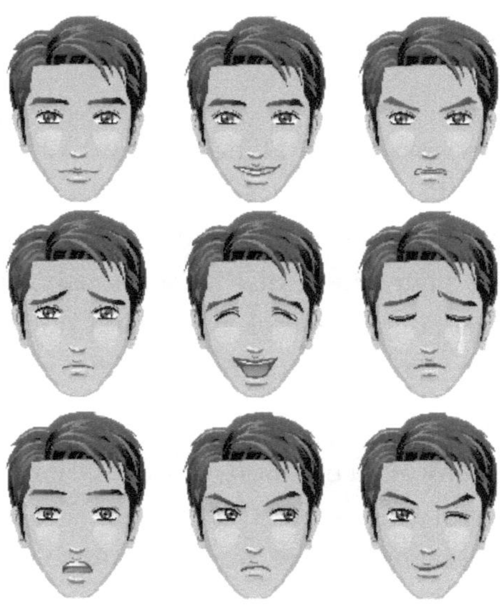

Art students do this as a mandatory practice. They sit in such crowded places, and try to draw as many faces as possible. This gives them the experience to observe and draw different kinds of faces quickly.

We don't have to draw those faces, just observing them and trying to guess what they are doing is enough. Once we are comfortable with this skill, we can go to the next step.

Now, try to observe people who are coming in a group. It may be a husband and wife, or a gang of youngsters, or a big family with kids running here and there. Try to pick one such group and observe their emotions in each person's face.

The difference between the earlier exercise and this is that you will now be able to see how people's emotions gel together, or resist each other. For example, a father who is angry with a child's behaviour may change his mind if the kid does something very smart. You can see this change in the parent's face instantly. This explains how one person's emotions are controlled by others' actions.

You can do the same at home too. For that, you would need comic books, or a television. Comic books are a great source of face reading. If you observe carefully, most of the comics will have many close-up pictures of various characters, with dialogues in one or two lines.

The good news is that these dialogues will explicitly say what the character feels, (for example: 'I don't like this nonsense') and at the same time, you will be able to match it with the drawing to see if your observation is correct or not.

Similarly, when television programmes, cartoons, movies or even sports programmes are shown, pick up the remote control and pause the screen when close-up shots of people/characters are shown. Try to guess what the emotion is on their face, and compare your answer with what actually happens on screen.

When you do such exercises regularly, you will become more and more confident in understanding others' emotions. Now you can slowly move away from the face, and start reading the next important aspect in people's feelings – body language!

Body Language

Just like our face, the rest of our body parts also constantly show emotions and express our feelings. Again, we may not realise it, but without opening our mouth, we can convey so much to the people we meet.

Fortunately, the reverse is also true. We can read the body language of everyone around us, and understand many things that they may not say explicitly.

There were some guests in Raj's home. They brought lot of sweets with them, and asked little Raj to have some. Raj was hesitant. He was not sure whether to accept those sweets or not.

True, the sweets were tempting, and he wanted to gobble all of them in one go. But that may make his mother angry and she may rebuke for his indecent behaviour.

So, he looks at his mother with pleading eyes, 'Can I accept these sweets Mommy?'

Raj's mother says, 'Sure dear, go ahead!'

Somehow, Raj is not convinced. He refuses to accept those sweets from the guests and runs away. Why?

The reason is very simple. Even though his mother asked him to accept those sweets, her body language suggested otherwise. It may be the eyes, or the posture, or the hands, or something else. But there was a hidden meaning which conveyed the message, 'Don't accept!'

Similar to Raj's mother, everyone we meet talk to us through their body. Even animals are known to follow these patterns, because they can't talk.

Body language is another psychological study which is very vast and beyond the scope of this book. But you can remember certain points, for reading the body language of people you meet:

- When someone adjusts their hair in front of you, it may mean they are trying to make themselves look more beautiful. On the other hand, it may also mean they are nervous and trying to self-assure themselves by touching.

- There are certain rules we follow when we shake our head. Left to right, or right to left usually means

'No,' up and down means 'Yes'. However, this may not be true universally, we need to be aware of the cultural differences and understand the head movements accordingly.

- Sometimes, when you are asking others about some work they were supposed to do, you can notice them touching the back of their head with their palms. This may be an indicator that they forgot to do it. Another similar indicator is, biting the tongue.

- When sitting, some people relax and recline in the back of the chair. Such people are usually confident about their role or position.

- Eye contact is very important in any communication. If someone doesn't look at you eye-to-eye during a conversation, it may mean he/she has done something wrong and is not able to face you. Another possibility could be that the person is not interested in whatever you are talking, and is trying to stay away from it.

- When people don't talk, look at their mouth. Some people purse their lips very strongly, this may mean they feel very strong about whatever they are saying, and don't want to comment about other things. On the other hand, talkative people will always have their mouth open, ready to jump into a discussion whenever they get a chance.

- Hands express many important things. For example, if a person extends his or her hands openly when talking to you, it may mean they are honest.

- During conversations, some people fold their hands close to their chest. This is considered a defensive move. That person doesn't want to face your words and is trying to hide behind his/her hands.

- Few people, especially those in high positions, keep their hands in their back, and join them to form a perfect "V" shape. This makes them stand in a straight posture and shows authority.

- A very obvious body language message is yawning. This means, 'I am feeling sleepy. When will you stop your lecture?'

Before you show this yawning signal, let me stop this list here. You can read more about body language from various other books. The trick is to use them effectively to understand others!

Emotion Pairs

There are two very interesting incidents, from the life of the great saint Swami Ramakrishna Paramahamsa.

One of his disciples, a young student, was walking towards the temple. On a street corner, there were few people discussing something animatedly.

When they saw this student, they immediately changed the topic of their discussion and called out, 'Hey youngman, aren't you from the ashram of Swami Ramakrishna?'

'Yes!'

They started laughing and commented, 'You are so young; why do you want to waste your time by following saints? Don't believe in your Swamiji, we feel he is a crook and not a Swamiji, after all.'

When they said this, the young man got very angry. He started shouting at them, 'Don't you dare talk about my Swamiji like this. I will not keep quiet listening to all your nonsense.'

At this, they all stopped their unsolicited advice. The young man was very happy and proud of what he had done. He went to the ashram and narrated the incident to Ramakrishna Paramahamsa.

Swamiji patiently listened to his story, and said, 'Son, What you did was wrong!'

The young man couldn't believe his ears. Tears rolled down his cheeks as he asked, 'Swamiji, please tell me what mistake I have done!'

'You are practising to become a saint. For that, you should have control over your mind. When those people told wrong things about me, you shouldn't have reacted the way you did. Instead, you should have calmly walked away from that place,' advised Ramakrishna Paramahamsa.

When he said those words, all the other disciples were also listening. Through this simple advice, they learnt a very important lesson on mind control.

A few days later, another disciple of Swamiji was travelling in a boat. Again, some people started criticising Ramakrishna Paramahamsa, raising baseless accusations against him.

Naturally, this disciple also got angry. But he didn't open his mouth because he remembered his teacher's advice and decided to control his mind.

After reaching the other side of the river, he went to his ashram. There he narrated the incident to Swami Ramakrishna Paramahamsa.

Again Swamiji said, 'Son, What you did was wrong!'

This young disciple was very surprised. 'Why Swamiji? I followed your advice sincerely!'

'Forget my advice. Those people are talking bad things about your teacher in your presence, isn't it your duty to raise objection? Why did you remain silent? You should learn to talk when there is injustice!'

Another swamiji, who saw both incidents went to Ramakrishna Paramahamsa and asked, 'Guruji, You gave a different advice on that day, and today you have changed your mind about a similar incident. Why?'

Ramakrishna Paramahamsa smiled and said, 'Incidents may be the same, but people are different. That's why I had to give a different advice this time!'

'I don't understand Guruji.'

'On that day, the disciple who shouted at those people was an angry young man, I advised him to be calm so that he can learn to control his mind.'

'But this young man is very soft by nature. If he remains soft, others may take advantage of him. So I advised him to react when something wrong happens in front of him.'

These two incidents, give us a very valuable lesson. So the lesson is that we may react differently to the same emotion (from others). It may depend on various factors such as the situation, seriousness of the problem, possible consequences, types of people involved, and so on.

To understand this better, let us do a small exercise called 'Locating Emotion Pairs'.

What is an 'Emotion Pair'?

As the name suggests, we will pair two emotions together. That means, for one emotion, the other becomes the reaction, and vice versa.

Confused? Let us see an example.

A boy is crying. What will his mother do to console him?

If he is hungry, she will feed him. If he is upset because his toy broke, she will assure him that she will get another toy. If he is crying due to a toothache, she will give him medicine to cure him or take him to a doctor.

Can you locate the pairs in this paragraph? For example, Hunger – Feeding … You can fill the rest.

Now, take the same discussion to emotions, feelings and how people react to different scenarios. Try to match the words in Set 1 (action), and Set 2 (reaction).

Set 1 (action)	Set 2 (reaction)
Happy	Distract
Sad	Break Ice
Angry	Console
Shy	Happy

Easy. Isn't it?

Not always. Like Ramakrishna Paramahamsa's disciples, sometimes we may face a scenario where the obvious reaction would be a wrong fit, and we need to think out-of-the-box before we can decide on how to react. Let us see a small incident to understand this difference better.

A boy is coming to school for the first time. He is very scared to leave his mother. In this situation, what will be the obvious reaction? Because the boy is afraid, the best reaction will be to do something to make him feel confident and at ease, so that he forgets his mother for a few hours.

But when we do it, we are forcibly ignoring the feelings of that little boy. We assume he will accept the ground realities of life, happily. It may be a very wrong assumption to make.

Hence, few schools think empathetically and adopt a different approach. They let the mother sit in the same classroom (or, just outside). This gives the child confidence that mother is always nearby. Slowly, the child moves away from the discomfort zone into a comfort area and starts liking the school. After that, no more cries in front of the school gate. He will happily send his mother back home!

Empathy is a very important tool to win hearts. Whether it is a school boy or an elderly gentleman, caring for them always touches them and binds you strongly!

Good Deeds

When I was in school, one of our teachers advised us to keep a small note book of 'good deeds'.

As the name suggests, we need to record all the good things we did everyday in that note. For example: 'Today I helped mom clean-up the kitchen', 'I guided an elderly man to cross the road', 'When the teacher was late, I monitored the class and ensured other class rooms were not disturbed' etc.

Boy scouts also maintain a similar 'good deeds' diary. In fact, they are supposed to do at least one good thing everyday.

From what you read in the last few paragraphs, can you define what a good deed is?

Today, I brushed my teeth. Later I ate breakfast. When coming to school, I carried my bag. Are these considered good deeds?

No. Why? Because you are the only person involved in these actions. By brushing your teeth, you only helped yourself. No one else was involved.

So what? Is doing good things for ourselves wrong?

Doing something good for yourself is on expected lines. That's why we normally don't count it as a 'good deed.' For a deed to be counted as 'good,' another person has to be involved. He or she should benefit from what you do, or both of you should share the benefit. Otherwise, it won't be termed a good deed.

Let us take a similar example. Your younger brother met with a small accident and is having trouble lifting anything by hand. So, you help him brush his teeth.

Do you see the difference? The moment another person (your brother) is involved, the whole scenario changes. In this case, you have understood the problems your brother is facing currently, and were empathetic towards him.

The same empathy is applicable to every good deed we do. When you see someone dropping their books on the road, immediately you feel for them, and help them gather those books. When your friend is upset over his/her low marks in the exam, you understand the pain, and offer to help him/her with the lessons for the next exam.

Such good deeds are very important in everyday life. Like the scouts, you can also maintain a note book where you record these. Alternatively, you can keep a common diary at home where every family member can record his or her good deeds everyday.

Three Steps

Ideally, showing empathy towards someone has three important steps:

- Understanding (How they feel)
- Recognition, Acceptance (I know how you feel)
- Reaction (without judgement…)

About the ways of understanding how others feel, we have already discussed face reading and body language concepts. There are many other methods like analysing the voice, posture, and other non-verbal clues which can help us in this.

But what if someone refuses to open-up, keeps his or her problem within, and we are not able to guess anything? There are no other options. We need to ask them, directly or indirectly.

People generally don't open-up easily. Most of them tend to keep their problems to themselves. Only few people would be expressive and discuss such intimate thoughts with others.

So, how do we make them talk?

Psychiatrists are specialists in the field, who talk to people on a regular basis, ask them the right questions and get the required answers.

We can also follow a similar strategy. Let us take a small example and see how questions can help us understand what is in the other person's mind.

A girl returns from school with a sad face. Seeing this, her mother gets upset and wants to know what went wrong.

'Honey, why are you looking dull? What happened?'

'Nothing!'

This means, there is definitely something that's disturbing her. She just doesn't want to open up. So, her mother decides to adopt a different strategy.

'Anything special in school? How were the classes? Did your teacher say something?'

'No!'

Again, a one-word answer — a road block. But mothers rarely lose patience, especially on such things. The next set of questions is shot at her.

'Did your friends do something? Did you hurt yourself while playing? Why don't you tell your mother? Don't you know I will help you to sort out issues, if any?'

Now, she starts talking. Complains loudly about something her friend did, and tears swell in her eyes. We are not worried about how her mother solved the problem. Just observe the way she framed the questions, assured her daughter that her feelings would be respected, and only then did the little girl start talking.

This feeling of comfort is very important. Unless and until we are sure the other person will understand our emotions and support us, we don't want to talk openly about anything. This is mainly because we are constantly afraid that others may not respect our feelings and will probably make a wrong judgement.

Breaking the ice is the first step in binding any relationship with empathy. If this doesn't happen, the other two steps of empathy cannot happen.

Remember, breaking this ice is not easy. In the beginning, the other person will look at you with doubtful eyes and try to give one word, non-committal answers to your questions.

If that happens, don't be angry with them or lose patience; if you care for the other person, you should be ready to spend the time and energy to ask further questions and make them talk.

The moment they start talking, acknowledge their emotions and listen to them attentively. Say things like 'I know how you must be feeling now', 'I can understand your frustration', 'I agree with you; in your situation, I would have done the same thing' and so on. Don't give any advise at this stage.

When acknowledging the other person's emotions, it may be a good idea to touch or hug the person. However, if you feel the other person doesn't like it for some reason or is not in such a state of mind, you can skip it.

After making them feel that you are on their side, you need to prove it. How? By simply supporting their feelings!

Of course, you may not be able to provide solutions to anything. But from your side, whatever little you can do would help and give them confidence.

In fact, many times what people need is, just a pair of ears to listen. They will tell you all they feel and get a great relief. This by itself will act as a consolation and prepare them to face their hurdles, head-on!

One point to remember is that these feelings are very personal. If someone talks to you about their inner feelings and emotions, it is only because they believe you as a true friend. Hence, it is your duty to ensure that you don't betray them.

Vivek and Uday were close friends. One day, Vivek told Uday, 'You know pal? I am very afraid of cockroaches!'

Uday was a very brave fellow. He showed great empathy and helped Vivek to overcome his fear of cockroaches.

After a few days, there was a silly fight in the school. As a result, Uday and Vivek parted ways, vowing never to speak to each other again.

Vivek was angered by this. He wrote on the blackboard in the class, 'UDAY WAS AFRAID OF COCKROACHES'.

You see the problem? Vivek has betrayed Uday's. Do you think Uday will ever open-up with anyone again?

Hearing vs. Listening

Rashmi's family was on a tour of Kashmir. Suddenly, Rashmi's younger brother fell ill and they took him to a nearby clinic. Rashmi's mother was very worried about her son's health. She kept talking non-stop on what could be the reason for his illness.

At one point, Rashmi's father got irritated and said, 'Stop this at once. Let the doctor examine the child and give his opinion.'

Rashmi's mother was silent for sometime and then started her nervous talks again. Exactly at that time, the doctor called them in.

After meeting the doctor, Rashmi's mother sounded very relieved. Now she was very confident that her son would recover very soon.

What happened? Did the doctor give some medicines to Rashmi's mother also? No. He just listened to her empathetically, and that was all she needed!

What has empathy to do with listening? As we saw in the last chapter, a majority of people are worried only because they have too many things in their mind. If they get a chance to talk to someone and express what they feel, it makes a huge difference for them. But unfortunately, not many people know how to listen.

It may sound silly, because listening is the easiest thing in this world. You don't even have to open your ears for that; they are already open. Just stand in front of the person who is talking and that's it – the words will go in automatically.

But what happens after that? Do they really reach your brain or not? That's what is more important. Think of it from the other person's perspective. If you listen to them attentively, they will be happy and be obliged to you for having respected their emotions and feelings. On the other hand, if you just hear the words and concentrate on some other work, they will feel insulted and ignored, and negative emotions would flow. This will be a real empathy killer!

So, what should we do? First, let us try to understand the difference between plain hearing, and listening.

For example, if your teacher shows great care to explain a concept that you do not understand the student–pupil relationship develops. Similarly, if your mother is busy doing the dishes, and your father offers to help, they develop a good understanding and love.

On the other hand, let us say you are reading a book which explains a concept with lovely diagrams... and you are able to understand the concepts clearly. In this case, only an information exchange takes place. As there is not a second person involved, there won't be any relationship or understanding.

In real-life scenarios, it is very easy for us to get into this trap and treat every interaction we have as pure information exchanges. If we react this way, the other person will feel hurt.

To convert a 'hear'ing session to a 'listen'ing experience, you need to follow certain ground rules. First among them is to 'be there'!

This means, when someone is talking seriously about their feelings, stop working on any other task. Be there, 100%. You might have seen some people talking to their guests with the television on. They will be listening, but their eyes will be fixed on the idiot box. This means, they don't really care for the other person's feelings. They are merely hearing, not listening.

If you want to listen, switch off the TV, computer monitor, stop doodling, don't adjust your shirt buttons, just look at the other person face-to-face and listen to what he/she is saying.

Next, don't judge them based on what they say. Just listen to their words, don't pass any judgment yet.

The topic may be boring to you, but for the sake of the person, be attentive. If possible, show your interest by saying things like 'I see', 'interesting', 'oh', 'I understand' etc. You can also use non-verbal indicators like nodding your head, body language, posture etc. While they are talking, don't interrupt, ask questions or stop them. Allow them to express their feelings and just listen.

Finally, after they have finished talking, it is time for you to say something. But be careful, the focus is still on them and on their issue. If you try to drag the attention to your side, they will feel upset.

Ponder over what they have said and find out if you are expected to give any suggestion or solution. Sometimes, mere listening would make the person feel at ease. This gives them a sense of comfort that someone is caring and concerned about them. But be careful not to be judgemental about the person or his emotions.

In many cases, the person who is talking to you just wants to say what is on mind. Beyond that the person doesn't expect any solution from you. But the problem is, not everyone understands this. Whenever people say anything to them, they jump to conclusions and give their (unsolicited) advice. It makes the other person very confused.

On the other hand, some people may approach you for genuine advice, 'I don't know how to come out of this mess; can you help me?'

This is an explicit request for solution or advice. In this case, we can offer one. Knowing the difference between the two is a very important lesson in empathy. If you don't handle it well, you may give advice when it is not solicited, or worse, remain silent when the other person looks forward to your solving the problem!

'Empathic Listening' or 'Active Listening' is a skill which needs a lot of practice. When you do it well, an environment of trust is created where emotions are released and managed effectively. This ensures a smoother decision making or problem solving!

Good Handle, Bad Handle

Is empathy a 'human' feeling?

This question has puzzled scientists and behaviour analysts for many years. They conducted various experiments to determine if animals show empathy towards fellow animals.

Few years back, Joan Silk, a famous primatologist, conducted one such experiment. He selected 18 chimpanzees and studied them. His team used a very interesting system to find out whether a chimpanzee cares for another unrelated animal or not.

They first placed a few chimpanzees (say, let us call them Group A) in separate cages. Next to each one of these chimpanzees, there were two handles – a good one, and a bad one.

If a chimpanzee pulled the good handle, it got some food. If it pulled the bad handle, it would still get the same amount of food.

So, what's the difference?

There was no difference, really. Irrespective of whichever handle the chimpanzee pulled, it got food!

Unlike many other animals, chimpanzees are closely related to humans. Hence, they were intelligent enough to find out soon, that the handles gave them food and enjoyed it.

On an average, these chimpanzees pulled both the 'good' and 'bad' handles equal number of times — roughly 50% each.

The researchers placed another group of chimpanzees (let's call these as Group B) in a cage with no handles and placed them opposite to the Group A chimpanzees.

As usual, Group A chimpanzees pulled the "good" handle, and surprisingly, animals from both the groups got food.

After some time, a chimpanzee from Group A pulled the "bad" handle, and only this chimpanzee got food. The animal from Group B didn't get anything.

Obviously, the other chimpanzee was very upset. It cried, shouted and banged on its cage walls. The Group A chimpanzee was watching all these, but didn't do anything.

By now, you would have understood the difference between "good" and "bad" handles. The good handle gave food to both chimpanzees, and the bad one gave food only to the chimpanzee that pulled it.

But Group A chimpanzees didn't think that way. Even though there was another chimpanzee in the next cage crying for food, it liked to pull both the good and the bad handles at equal intervals. This means, it didn't care for the other chimpanzee at all. There is no sign of empathy here.

Considering the fact that chimpanzees have very close relationship with humans, will the same experiment work if men and women are used instead of animals?

Another group worked on this. They decided to use supermarket consumers to gauge their empathy levels. For this, a volunteer stood at a prime spot in a busy supermarket, with a note which said, 'Free chocolates.'

Obviously, a crowd gathered around this volunteer and everyone asked him, 'Where is my free chocolate?'

The volunteer smiled and said, 'I will give you the free chocolate. But before that, can you answer one simple question?'

'Yes, but make it short, please!'

'I will give you two choices. In one, only you get a free chocolate, and in the second choice, both you and I get free chocolates. Which option you would choose?'

The consumers thought for a moment, and almost all of them chose option 2. If you compare the chimpanzee experiment with this, you can clearly see the similarities, and of course the differences. While chimpanzees chose not to help the other animal even when it cost them nothing, human beings behave differently. They tend to help fellow humans when there is a choice.

This is only a small example. In our day-to-day life, we do so many actions driven by empathy. Consider this simple example: when we see a stranger in a bus, we offer the seat next to us. Why? What do we get out of it? Nothing.

By nature, we like helping others and care for fellow human beings. This is a very important step in understanding human behaviour!

Sympathy & Empathy

Two friends were sitting in a park on a bench. A blind person came to them and asked for some help. The first person searched through his pocket and gave him a one-rupee coin. But the second person gave the blind man a crisp hundred-rupee note.

Obviously, his friend was surprised, 'I know you are kind to people, a hundred rupee for a beggar? Isn't it a bit too much?'

The second person smiled and said, 'It's because I feel for him. I understand his problems and feel like helping him. Is there anything wrong in it?'

His friend was not convinced. 'We have been friends for twenty years; I have never seen you being so generous with any beggar. There must be some other reason, tell me!'

'Okay, I will tell you. But let me warn you first. It's a long story.'

'No problem, I have all the time in the world!'

'Do you remember? A few weeks back, I went to Goa on an official trip. My company took care of the travel arrangements. But when I reached there, someone stole my purse.'

'Oh! My god!'

'I was shocked. Fortunately, my stay, food and all other needs were already taken care of. But I felt like a begger, without a penny.'

'So, what did you do?'

'What else? I was forced to ask for a loan from the hotel. I promised to pay back as soon as I got some cash from my office.'

'Did they help you?'

'No. That's the saddest part. Even though I stayed there for a week or so and my entire bill, running to many thousands, was settled by my company beforehand, they didn't believe me. They politely refused to give me any cash in advance. After that, I had to do a lot of juggling till I got some cash, and saved myself from this big mess.'

'So, that's what made you show empathy towards the poor, who face problems because of the lack of money, right?'

'Yes!'

'Dear friend, don't misunderstand me. I guess you are confused. Your feeling towards that beggar is sympathy, not empathy!'

So what is the difference?

Sympathy and empathy are very different from each other. When you are sympathetic, you pity them or feel sorry for them. You don't understand the exact feeling of the person and are left with little choice. You may extend a physical or monetary support but it may not be the solution for every person or their problem.

On the other hand, empathy is 'feeling with the person'. You are placing yourself in that person's place, understand what they feel and sharing their emotions.

Sympathy is when you feel bad for someone else. Empathy is when you feel bad with someone else.

Now you can clearly see the difference. In case of this person who gave a hundred-rupee note to a beggar, he started feeling for poor people, after he lost his money in Goa. He felt like a beggar once. It made him feel for the other person as if it was he who was suffering. That makes it a sympathetic relationship.

It is very important that we realise this fine line between sympathy and empathy in life, and use sympathy only when it is absolutely necessary. Otherwise, empathy gives you everything you need to feel for, and help others!

EQ

Ahmed was a very bright student. Unlike many other kids of his age, he loved attending school and enjoyed classrooms much more than playgrounds. Naturally he did well in all his exams and always stood first in his class.

But in one of the class tests he scored just 80 marks in Mathematics. He was very upset. You may think 80 is a decent score. But it was not so for Ahmed who was used to getting 100/100. Anything below that was simply not acceptable to him.

So the class teacher called Ahmed and asked him, 'What's wrong Ahmed? I have never seen you so upset. Can I help you?'

'I am not sure Ma'am. As usual, I had prepared well, but during the exam something strange happened which affected my performance.'

'What was that?'

'We had 2 hours for completing the test. After an hour I realized that I was still left with more than half of the question paper. This got me worried. I wasn't able to concentrate and I left a few questions unanswered.'

The teacher patted him and said, 'Don't worry Ahmed. It's not your mistake; you need to improve your EQ.'

'EQ? You mean IQ, right?'

'No. Your IQ is very good. What you are lacking is EQ, or Emotional Intelligence Quotient. Emotional Intelligence is the ability to handle one's feelings and it is measured in terms of Emotional Intelligence Quotient. Emotional intelligence helps you to understand yourself, and also helps you to understand the feelings and emotions of others.'

During the exam, when Ahmed looked at the watch, an emotion (fear or anxiety) took him off guard and it was dominating him for the next one hour. When that happened, his IQ didn't help. So Emotional Quotient is crucial for his development.

A person with a high emotional quotient will become more responsible and respectful. He will have an increased ability to show empathy, and find it easier to develop self restraint. On the other hand, a person with a low emotional intelligence will often feel helpless.

You might have seen people getting angry at everything. On the other hand, there are people who control their anger pretty well and use it effectively. Whom do you think will be more successful?

Putting in simple terms, Emotional Intelligence is nothing but the ability to express and control our emotions based on various life scenarios. The challenge is whether your logical / rational thought process or your emotions control your actions.

Okay. But which one is better-- Logical thinking or emotional thinking? In other words, should we think with our brain, or heart?

There is no definite answer to this question as it depends on many factors.

For example, should you eat a burger or a salad?

Thinking logically, salad is a wiser and a healthier choice. But our taste buds control our emotions and make us choose the burger instead. This may be okay once in a while, but if we make it an everyday choice, it can become a health issue.

This is why we need a good balance of IQ and EQ. At any given point of time we should be able to think rationally at the same time let our emotions control the show when it is necessary. If it does not work, keep them on the backseat and let the logical thought process take over.

So what should we do to have a better EQ? There are some very simple suggestions given by researchers, psychologists and behavioural analysts.

1. Before reacting to any action or situation, spend few minutes analyzing the problem from various angles, the possible options and the respective results. Make a decision accordingly using rational thought process or deal with it emotionally.

2. Evaluate your behaviour regularly – May be you can make it your last activity of the day, just before going to bed. Ask yourself: How did I react to various situations I faced today? What are the good / bad lessons? Did I see things from others' perspective and act with empathy? If not, why? Given a chance, how will I do it different next time? Should I apologize for the (intentional/ unintentional) mistakes I did today? How?

If these two suggestions are constantly followed your EQ will improve in a pace faster than your IQ.

Yale psychologist, Peter Salovey, has identified the following five areas to improve one's emotional intelligence:

- **Know your emotions:** Work on increasing the ability to recognize a feeling as it happens.

- **Regulate your emotions:** Improve your ability to handle feelings and to recover quickly from upsets and distress.

- **Motivate yourself:** Learn to collect your emotions in order to reach goals. Apply self-control and self-discipline.

- **Cultivate empathy:** Try to recognize, identify, and feel what others are feeling.

- **Manage relationships.** Respond appropriately and in helpful ways to the feelings of others.

Researches show that an emotionally intelligent person is far more successful than a person with a high Intelligent Quotient. In a long term basis, this could also change your whole life for good!

Eight Desires

In the previous chapter, we saw how important it is for us to adjust our emotional behaviour according to the situation we are in.

It doesn't stop there. Sometimes we may have to change our emotional behaviour based on the people we are dealing with. We already saw an example from Ramakrishna Paramahamsa's life on how this can be done.

But how do we apply this principle in our everyday behaviour? Are there any rules that help us determine what kind of people we work with?

UK-based Empathy Training Limited has put forward a very effective tool for this purpose. This is based on various psychological research findings.

According to this tool, 90% of our emotional behaviour comes from just seven inner drives or desires. This understanding can be used to find out our own emotional needs, as well as that of others whom we interact with.

Before we write down those seven desires, it is important that we set a clear ground rule. These shouldn't be used to label people on a permanent basis. This is because most of the time you and I will be a mix of these seven types. No one will be #3 or #5 or #6 forever, but a combination of these based on the situation.

Also, there are certain desires named after typical professions like 'Engineer', 'Artist' etc. But this doesn't mean that the person has studied engineering, or is dealing with a paint brush. We use these terms to explain their behaviour — they should be taken as simple examples only.

Now let us enumerate those seven basic desires, or inner drives here.

Normal

As the name suggests, this is where many of us stay most of the time. These people want to keep everything in order, don't like expressing too much joy or infact any other emotions. They want to think, behave and argue logically, follow rules, regulations, laws. They feel that their life is their own responsibility and like to take control of it.

To summarise, there is nothing special or exceptional about this first 'inner drive'. Being normal, we feel the society will accept us. To ensure this, our emotional behaviour will follow rational, logical rules and it's a lot easier to predict someone's behaviour when they are in this state of mind.

Hustler

The word 'hustle' means pushing, or making way. Hustlers make sure that they succeed, always. According to them, there are no exceptions to this rule, and failure is never an option!

Of course, there is nothing wrong in trying to succeed all the time. But hustlers ensure that their own goals are met, even if it is at the expense of someone else's failure.

It's not fair, but that's how the human mind works at times. For hustlers material success is more important than anything else. They are very proud of their possessions, they think money is more important than all other things put together. They don't mind taking a risk or two to achieve success, get money, fame, and several other luxuries in life.

Mover

These people like to move things a bit, and are always active and dynamic. They show initiative in whatever they do, start working on many things, pull people around them for support, and so on.

But unfortunately, these people are not known to be finishers. This means, they soon lose focus on many things they start, and move on to start off other things. They easily get distracted, mainly because they always like doing something new. Old things that need maintenance, tinkering, and a repair or two bore them.

Based on this, you can guess how their emotions are. It's always like a roller-coaster, moving up and down, from active to inactive, interest and disinterest. It's all part of their game.

Double Checker

The process of 'double-check' means, checking anything twice (or more) to ensure it is completed properly. For example, after writing an essay, such people read it twice, just to make sure there are no errors or factual mistakes. Even when they lock a door, they wouldn't be satisfied until they try to open the door themselves and ensure that the lock works.

The reason for such double checking is security. These people always imagine problems (realistic and unrealistic). They feel that the chances of a problem occurring are higher than normal and hence, there is nothing wrong in being extra cautious.

For example, when they travel to a warm place, they may pack their raincoat. The rationale is, 'what if it rains?'

This 'what if' and 'in case' thoughts drive them to keep all options open. They are always confused.

We have to be extremely cautious if we meet such persons because if we try to advice them, it usually doesn't solve their problem. Instead, our option puts them to another dilemma by opening the door to many other alternatives to worry about.

Artist

The term 'art' doesn't really mean paintings and drawings alone. Even sculptors, actors, musicians and the like are called artists. So we are trying to use that broader term here.

Artists are known to be creative people. They don't like following the crowd and would prefer to create a new path for themselves.

Due to this nature, artists are full of ideas. They are able to visualise any problem, and arrive at a conclusion which not only solves the issue but is also a very creative, never-tried-before idea.

However, there is a catch here. Because of their artistic thought process, these people open-up realistic and unrealistic ideas in almost equal numbers. And they won't be able to differentiate between what will work and what won't. According to them anything should work. They are motivated by the thought, 'Why not?'

When we work with artists, we need to remember their desire to be different. Most of the artists are very sensitive and shy. They don't make friends very easily, but the rare friendships they make, usually lasts longer.

Politician

In a way, the politician's desire is similar to that of a hustler. These people also want to win, at any cost!

The important personality trait of this group is the desire to lead. In any crowd, they emerge as natural leaders and provide solutions, guidance etc. They have a charismatic appearance and excel in communication, and are able to attract followers naturally.

These people have opinions on everything – be it an international problem, or a local next-door issue. They have an opinion, and are very strong at expressing them. If anyone disagrees with them, politicians like to debate the issue and arrive at a conclusion, rather than agreeing to disagree.

Due to this nature, many times they are seen as adamant people. It may be very difficult for anyone to change their views and policies, even if the argument is very logical and strong!

Engineer

You may be aware of the famous saying, 'engineers make the world'. That's the essence of this seventh and final desire in our list.

Engineers like to take up anything as a mission and drive themselves towards its completion. They may be purchasing a house, or simply trying to find a place to eat that night. They take up everything as a serious project and work towards achieving the end results with minimal hassles.

According to engineers, any project includes requirements, a process, a proper plan and deliverables. They would like to set these rules straight before starting to work on anything.

When the requirements are detailed out, engineers like to take detailed notes so that they will be able to use this information as a foundation for future work. Based on this data, they plan their activities and execute the plan properly.

Unlike movers, engineers don't like to work on different things at the same time. One project, or better, one task at a time works perfect for them, and any further pressure may push them to an uncomfortable zone.

Most of the engineers are hands-on people. Even if tasks are delegated to their peers or subordinates, or a third party, they would still like to roll-up their sleeves and work.

This causes certain conflicts among team members, because they might feel that engineers are disturbing 'their' work. But in such scenarios, others should understand that engineers like taking ownership only for a complete project. They are only willing to help, as all are moving towards the same goal.

To summarise these seven inner drives, you, I and everyone around us are at times normal, sometimes success-craving hustlers, sometimes active and dynamic movers, and sometimes security-conscious double checkers. At times we are creative artists, sometimes power-crazy politicians and even project-oriented engineers. This diverse set of personalities is what makes relationships very interesting.

Hence, when we express empathy towards a friend, family member, fellow worker, or even a stranger ask yourself: among these inner drives, which state of mind this person is currently in, what makes him or her behave this way? By expressing my emotions (due to empathy) now, will I be disturbing that equation? Based on these thoughts, you will be able to come to an optimal decision and execute it effectively.

Empathy may be very useful in many places: schools, offices, shops, service centers, when we speak to others over a phone, customer service scenarios, medical care centers and so on. This changes the face of human interaction a lot and creates a positive impact.

That's why many corporations have identified the immediate and serious need to embed empathy in their employee's everyday interaction with co-workers, customers, and others. Most of the companies have setup empathy training programs for new recruits, as well as existing customer-service employees.

Remember, empathy is not something which can be taught very effectively. You can read books, listen to lectures, watch video programmes on empathy, but at the end of the day, your mind should have the prerequisites to feel for another person. If this is missing, no amount of training can help you.

Luckily, as we saw in the chimpanzee example, the human brain is wired to express empathy with fellow beings, and it is only natural that we show it. Make sure you don't lose this treasure, at any cost!

www.ingramcontent.com/pod-product-compliance
Lightning Source LLC
LaVergne TN
LVHW040050180726
843489LV00003B/1113